This book belongs to

_____

Sam Walton

By Mary Nhin

Illustrated By
Yuliia Zolotova

This book is dedicated to my children - Mikey, Kobe, and Jojo.

Copyright © 2022 by Grow Grit Press LLC. All rights reserved. No part of this book may be reproduced in any form without permission in writing from the publisher. Please send bulk order requests to growgritpress@gmail.com Printed and bound in the USA. MiniMovers.tv
Paperback ISBN: 978-1-63731-638-2

Hi, I'm Sam Walton.

Growing up, my days almost always began at 4:30am. I helped my family by working multiple jobs - delivering newspapers, selling magazine subscriptions, and milking cows.

I believed in working hard at everything I did. For fun, I played high school football and basketball, helping my teams get to the championships.

My classmates voted me "Most Versatile Boy".

MOST VERSATILE BOY

After high school, I went to the University of Missouri and then worked for JCPenney, a retail store.

Around this time, I met my wife, Helen, and we got married on Valentine's Day.

In 1942, I resigned from my job, so that I could serve in the army for my country, eventually becoming a captain.

When you're serving in the military, you get a lot of time to think. It was there that I knew I wanted to pursue retail. So that's exactly what I did when I got back to regular life.

I purchased a Ben Franklin variety store in Newport, Arkansas.

5¢ AND 10¢ BEN FRANKLIN

"Thanks for loaning me $20,000, Dad."

"You're welcome, Sam. I believe in you."

With my very own store, I had the freedom to test out my concepts. I learned and improved by trial and error. Here's a couple of things I learned early on:

- If I offered prices as good or better than stores in cities that were four hours away by car, people would shop at home.
- Offering a wide range of goods made my customers happy.

The attention to detail really paid off and my sales almost tripled! I was happy that all was going well!

But then my landlord told me he wouldn't renew my lease and I could no longer operate there. He secretly wanted the store to keep for his son!

I had to pick myself up and get on with it, do it all over again, only even better this time.

I was sad I had to find another location, but this was a very early business lesson for me to learn.

While many of the existing retail stores only opened in big cities, I dared to be different by opening in small towns.

I negotiated the purchase of a small discount store in Bentonville, Arkansas, but only if I got a 99-year lease to expand into the shop next door.

The owner of the shop next door refused six times, but in one final attempt my father-in-law paid the shop owner a final visit and $20,000 to secure the lease. I had just enough left from the sale of the first store to close the deal, and reimburse my father-in-law.

My brother, Bud, and I opened more Ben Franklin franchises, 16 in total. We even learned how to fly an airplane so that we could get from store to store.

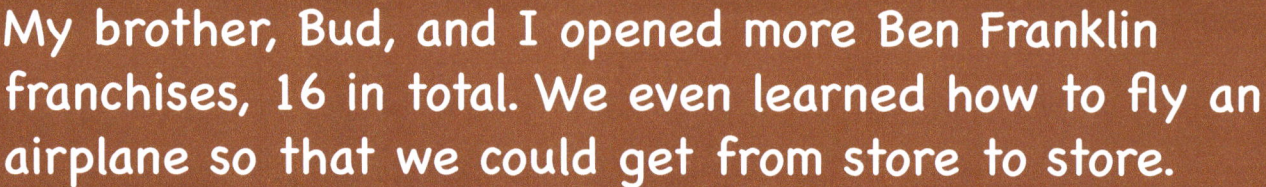

When we didn't agree on expansion and growth strategies with the leaders at Ben Franklin, I decided it was time to open our very own retail store - Wal-Mart.

The very first store opened on July 2, 1962. The rest is history.

By 1991, Walmart Inc. became the nation's largest retailer, with 1,700+ stores. In 1997, our company had over $100 billion in sales.

Even though I was successful, I still preferred to get my hair cut for $5.

If I could leave you one piece of advice, it would be:

Swim upstream. Go the other way. Ignore the conventional wisdom.

Timeline

1942 - Sam is inducted into U.S. Army.

1945 - Sam opens his first Ben Franklin five-and-dime franchise.

1962 - Sam opens first Wal-Mart.

1969 - Wal-Mart is incorporated.

1991 - Wal-Mart becomes the nation's largest retailer, with 1,700 stores.

1997 - Wal-Mart surpasses $100 billion in sales.

minimovers.tv

 @marynhin   @officialninjalifehacks
#minimoversandshakers

 Mary Nhin   Ninja Life Hacks

 Ninja Life Hacks

 @officialninjalifehacks

www.ingramcontent.com/pod-product-compliance
Lightning Source LLC
Chambersburg PA
CBHW041521070526
44585CB00002B/33